BLAME MONTEZUMA!

BLAME
MONTEZUMA!

*An Assortment
of
Chocolate Poems*

Happen*Stance*

Acknowledgements:
Sue Butler's 'Hunger' is from her Happen*Stance*
pamphlet *Arson*, 2011; 'Terry's', by Donald Mackay, was
in his Mariscat Press pamphlet *On Time*, 2012; 'The
Emigration Game', by Gerda Mayer, first appeared in
The Observer Review in 1989, is now in her book
Bernini's Cat (Iron Press, 1999) and has been widely
anthologised; Helena Nelson's 'Dip Me in Chocolate
and Throw me to the Lesbians' first appeared in *Ambit*
175, 2004; 'Drinking Hot Chocolate in the Rain', by
Robert Nye, is in his collection *An Almost Dancer,
Poems 2005-2011* (Greenwich Exchange, 2012); Stephen
Payne's 'Easter' was in the ezine *Flashquake*, 4,3, Spring
2005; Pauline Prior-Pitt's '70%' was included in her 2013
collection *Elsewhere* (Spike Press); N S Thompson's
'Chocolate on a Sunday Night' first appeared in *New
Walk,* 6, Spring/Summer 2013.

Printed and bound in the UK by
Berforts Information Press, Stevenage

Published in 2014 by Happen*Stance*
21 Hatton Green, Glenrothes, Fife KY7 4SD
www.happenstancepress.com

CONTENTS

'Is this a whole new genre, then?'

R S KING, Limerick / 11

NOEL WILLIAMS, Out of the Box / 12

ALISON CAMPBELL, Choc-Lit /13

JAMES HENDERSON-FINDLAY, Dear Mrs Barker / 14

JO FIELD, On the Brief Pause Before Eating a Box of Chocolates / 15

DI COFFEY, Regeneration / 16

MARTIN PARKER, Macbeth Fails to Give Up Chocolate / 17

GILL MCEVOY, Creed / 18

ALAN HILL, Her Dark Sublime / 19

TERRY QUINN, After Three Pints on New Year's Eve / 20

'Mokaya tribes concocted xocolātl'

JOANNA WATSON, Mesoamerican Beginnings / 23

ROY MARSHALL, Nestlé, Pallanza, 1940 / 24

ANNIE FISHER, Five Boys (1902-1976) /25

GINA WILSON, 'Mild Dessert' / 26

GERDA MAYER, The Emigration Game / 27

JENNY ELLIOTT, Chocolate Night / 28

N S THOMSON, Offering on a Sunday Night / 30

PAULINE PRIOR-PITT, Craving / 31

STEPHEN PAYNE, Easter / 32

DAVID HALE, Memory / 33

C J DRIVER, Inside / 34

'Chocolate has it'

ROSE COOK, It / 37

VIVIEN JONES, Valentine's Recipe on *Woman's Hour* / 38

OLIVER COMINS, Your Fingers on my Cellophane /39

DOROTHY BAIRD, Music of the Squares / 40

PAULINE PRIOR-PITT, 70% / 41

JOANNE MCKAY, Temptation / 42

GILL LEARNER, Advice to a Gentleman Caller / 43

TONY CLOKE, Loss / 44

JANET LOVERSEED, The Ladies from the Slimming Club
    Wear Black / 45

EDITH RYAN, Perfect Picture / 46

'Irrefutable proof that contraries co-exist'

MARCIA MENTER, Salt-Caramel Logic / 49
ALISON BRACKENBURY, Bournville Babies / 50
JIM C WILSON, Dark Choku / 51
JOANNA GRIGG, Evidence of Kindness / 52
HILARY MENOS, Wakusei Shokora / 53
MIKE MUNRO, Good for Something / 54
DAVID MARK WILLIAMS, Bath / 55
JO FIELD, I'll say I don't like chocolate / 56
SUE BUTLER, Hunger / 57
JENNIFER COPLEY, Their Angel / 58

'Crudbury's, Milk Decay, Quality Shite'

MARY WIGHT, Rest / 61
ROB A MACKENZIE, Chocolate Dream from Sheol / 62
DONALD MACKAY, Terry's / 63
HELEN EVANS, Chocoholic / 64
MARTIN ZARROP, Trade / 65
HELENA NELSON, 'Dip me in chocolate and throw me
    to the lesbians' / 66
HELEN ADDY, Rita Black / 67
TOM DUDDY, Trove / 68

'It used to be cocoa'

CLARE BEST, Hot Chocolate at Baratti's / 71
JOHN PURSER, Bedtime / 72
ENID LEE, The Word / 73
CLIFFORD FORDE, Ode / 74
ANITA JOHN, After Sledging / 75
ROSS KIGHTLY, Being grown-up is / 76
MATTHEW STEWART, Chocolate con Churros / 77
ROBERT NYE, Drinking Hot Chocolate in the Rain / 78

BLAME MONTEZUMA!

*'Is this a whole new
genre, then?'*

R S King

Limerick

Chocolate chocolate chocolate
Chocolate chocolate chocolate
Chocolate chocolate
Chocolate chocolate
Chocolate chocolate chocolate

Noel Williams

Out of the Box

You brush your lips. I meet your glance.
While no-one sees, come—take your chance.

My ribbon's slipped. My lid's askew.
Deep in my foil, who'll miss a few?

Let fingers roam my strawberry creams
ripe with your tongue's forbidden dreams.

Here! Touch me. Squeeze like CPR.
Raise up my rich montelimar.

Bite my rough nougat with your teeth.
Though plain above, I'm dark beneath.

Alison Campbell

Choc-Lit

I want a chocolate poem, she said.
You can make it plain
but not too dark
though you mustn't fudge the issue
and please, don't be flaky,
hard-core, soft-centred
or nutty.

I see, I said.
Is this a whole new genre, then?

James Henderson-Findlay

Dear Mrs Barker

I have filled my printer cartridges
with 70% dark chocolate so that

when you have received and read
this letter, printed as it is

on rice paper, I can invite you
to eat it—but not the envelope,

printed with 100% black toner
(if our addresses were chocolate

the Royal Mail would not survive:
all would be consumed

and nothing would arrive).

Jo Field

On the Brief Pause Before Eating
a Box of Chocolates

Might I compare it to a summer's day?
The kind of summer that we used to have:
hours like elastic waistbands, comfortably
expanding to a perfect fit. Above,
the sun always apparent; under it
a depth of grass which you could sink into . . .
while everywhere the birds would sing for you
of some glad future with your name on it.

Open the box!
                 Discard the printed key
and its redundant words—*enrobed? oozing?*
Relish that keen olfactory thrill and be
content to let blind fingers do the choosing.
Submerge yourself in soft anticipation—

soon you will know the joy of wild gustation.

Di Coffey

Regeneration

In fanciful moments
I revive my county's fortune

down mocha-scented tunnels
in chocolate mines

bringing orange crème
to apple-cheeked bal maidens

who tap and sell
Cornwall's centre

to drooling tourists
queuing round the coastline

Martin Parker

Macbeth Fails to Give Up Chocolate

Chocolate that knits up the ravelled sleeve of care,
Balm of hurt minds, great nature's second course

And that which should accompany old age,
I have thee not and yet I see thee still.

Proceeding from the heat-oppressèd brain
Methought I heard a voice cry, 'Eat no more'.

Throw physic to the dogs! Lay on the stuff
And damned be him who first cries, 'Hold, enough!'

Gill McEvoy

Creed

My life-support, my friend indeed,
stalwart stay in times of need,

henchman in my times of greed,
I have really gone to seed

because of you.

Feed me chocolate, I plead.
My life-support, my friend in deed.

Alan Hill

Her Dark Sublime

Whenever denied the hot jollies of gender
Lavinia Bottral would go on a bender,
devouring dark chocolate in myriad forms,
her consumption exceeding respectable norms.

En fin she'd lie down (once her craving was sated
and the fires of visceral lust had abated),
comfortably curled in a posture near-foetal,
enjoying an afterglow quasi-coital.

Terry Quinn

After Three Pints on New Year's Eve

sometimes
the harder the resolution
the easier it is
while merely saying
I might eat less
70% dark chocolate
made with the finest Trinitario
cocoa beans for an intense taste and
certified to Soil Association standards
for food and farming
has me scouring cupboards

and seconds later
the *Oxford English*
a promise is a promise
a resolution's a separation of components
a proposal to a meeting
a resolution is the removing of doubt
so if there's doubt
then I'm removing it
by making a resolution not to

I like to think that's reason

'*Mokaya tribes concocted xocolātl*'

Joanna Watson

Mesoamerican Beginnings

Chocolate was born as beans
in pods of *Theobroma cacao,*
food of gods, machete-lopped
from forest understory—

fermented, roasted, kibbled, winnowed,
ground to liquor, blended to entice.
Mokaya tribes concocted *xocolātl,*
cacao beans with chilli, *bitter water.*

Aztec priests placated Quetzalcoatl,
plumed snake god, with cocoa tributes,
chocolate-imbibing rituals.
Conquered nations tendered beans as tax.

One bean would buy a large tomato,
three an avocado, four a pumpkin,
ten a rabbit or a harlot's services.
A slave was worth one hundred.

Conquistador Cortés acquired
plantations, seeded Spanish trade
converting beans to chocolate—
sweetened, fattened food of Mammon.

Roy Marshall

Nestlé, Pallanza, 1940

My Nonna smuggled sugar in her underwear
past the overseer, wheeling her bike over the bridge
where the German guards walked back and forth,
boy-faced under steel helmets.

Nestlé and Nonna both survived the war,
and after decades by the chattering conveyer
they gave her a discount on bars bought in bulk.

Stacked like bullion, scenting the darkness
of the wooden cupboard, unwrapped and snapped
onto *Michette* for four o'clock *Merenda*, shining squares
nestled on the ripped white bread.

[*Michette*: bread rolls, *Merenda*: after school snack]

Annie Fisher

Five Boys (1902-1976)

'*Desperation, Pacification, Expectation,*
Acclamation, Realisation'

Such precision in the calibration,
the itemisation and nominalisation,
the frame-by-frame forensic revelation
of his count-down to transfiguration

but then this was a generation
that savoured verbose explanation,
relished polysyllabic proliferation
and could correctly spell accomodation

one that could defer gratification
and read the wrapper first for information,
knowing lexical procrastination
heightens tantalisation

increasing salivation
at the point of mastication,
giving rise to consolation
that defies articulation.

[*Five Boys* was a chocolate bar made by Fry's—later Cadbury's. The
wrapper featured five photo-portraits of the same small boy in a sailor
suit displaying a range of emotions from tearful misery to the bliss of
chocolate 'realisation'.]

Gina Wilson

'Mild Dessert'

Behind the raised sheets of his paper, with only his knees
and neat feet showing, sits Father, the sacrosanct tranches
laid out, just so, on his chair-arm. She watches a faint bloom

form on their not-milk, not-bitter, skins; waits
for the click of teeth on pipe-stem, the curl of smoke-signals
perfectly spaced. On cue, his hand glides out

by itself to the nearest slice, snaps off
a line of squares, retreats. She can hear him behind
his screen, hard at his ritual feast: sweet, secret

tie to the good thing that happened once—lucky chance
that whisked him from home to learn mild manners, new voice,
how to hide, maybe how to grow rich. A Cadbury's scholar

at Cambridge. He's not lucky now; no-one tells her why.
Father's chocolate makes her mouth water, the riches of classy,
refined bars, exposed but not offered. Later

he'll rewrap what's left in its turquoise and gold and set it
beside the green Gallaher tin on his desk. She has others,
old empties, secretly lodged in the hedge for kids

to leave notes in (if they remember), sometimes a sweet.
They know she's not allowed out on Sundays. She hears them
like birds in the lane, their squabbles and spurts of song.

Gerda Mayer

The Emigration Game

Winter 1938/1939

Mother and I walk through the streets of Prague.
Her hands are balled against the falling snow.
(Can't she afford gloves? Are they bare from choice?)
There's snow above and endless steps below.

We have a bag of chocolate-creams. We play
The Emigration Game: England, if brown,
Or, if the centre's white, we must stay here.
If yellow, it's Australia. Snow falls down.

I pick a brown and mother has the white.
She walks with a straight back: *Let's try again.*
Her legs are varicosed; her heels are raised.
She's bearing up and stout of heart. In vain

From consulate to consulate her steps
Inscribe petitions. Soon the sweets are gone.
Then March comes and invaders bar all routes
Yet leave no trace of her when they move on,

Their footsteps beating time and bearing down.

Jenny Elliott

Chocolate Night

To reach that exquisite place
everything has to be just so.
It's complicated.

I do my research.

The *criollo* bean is best,
bean of the Maya, of nights
aromatic, intense and rare

and the pods must be ripe
before cutting, with sweet pulp
clinging to their seeds:

fermentation needs sugar.
Then comes drying, cleaning,
roasting and grinding, liquefying . . .

I can go there now.

I am sitting in the back seat of the car
and I am very young. There are lights:
headlights, street lights, shop lights . . .

There is separation
of cocoa butter from cocoa solids
and then blending again.

. . . lights held in the blackness,
in the rain spread on the windscreen,
the wipers beating on and on.

The mix is what matters
and there is something important
about crystal size.

Petula Clark is singing.

Her face is slowly spinning,
the lights are much brighter there
and she's waiting for me tonight.

It's complicated,
but the conching and the tempering
will see to it.

I am very small
and right now my parents are happy.
I know a song called *Downtown*

and it wraps itself around us,
holding us together,
making everything just so.

N S Thompson

Offering on a Sunday Night

They were a mystery, these things above
Us, as we left the table and the world of tea
    Behind us—so strained in its silence we
Could cut it with a knife—and glimpsed the glowing reds
    Outside, a rubric of suspension dots,
The streetlamps smouldering in the gathering dusk as we
    Set off on sortie, quickmarched to the grim
Main road that marshalled districts to the onslaught of
    A great metropolis, its rank and file
Of empty streets stretched lifeless, uniform and grey,
    Until a neon pub sign shot against
A wall, its sleepy series of repeats winked to
    A bathroom window bathed in yellow light;
But we were kept in line, heads bowed towards the crisp
    Cold pavement, profiles low, as if the sight
Of three intruders in the curfew quiet could
    Be caught by fishing eyes as lights came on
With televisions after tea and one man flanked
    By his two small fry slipped the networks of
A no-mind-land beneath the rosy beads
    Of tracer as they made it to the line
Of shops and shining newsagent's; and there we crossed
    To wait outside against the windowpane
Until he came out with the bag of sweets, the sparks
    Of glassy neon pomegranate seeds
Now yellow boughs where bright mimosa hung and two
    Small minds were struck that only chocolates
Could soften up the brittleness we felt at home
    And prayed that we could take them quietly
And bring some peace as we shot down the pavements, our
    Hands round the offering on a Sunday night.

Pauline Prior-Pitt

Craving

Now she's settled in her bed
it's half past ten
and she's having an early night

and now she's running downstairs
and emptying her handbag
and opening every drawer

and now she's opening cupboards
and climbing onto chairs
searching on the top shelves

and now she's running upstairs
pulling off her nightie
and putting on her clothes

and now she's running downstairs
unlocking the front door
and running to her car

and now she's speeding six miles
out along the ring road
to the late night garage

and now she's tearing at the wrapper
breaking off a big piece
and cramming it into her mouth

Stephen Payne

Easter

Rise early and before the day begins
go traipsing, bleary-eyed, around the house,
putting aside the quarrels of last night
and remembering similar mornings;
their discoveries might help you now
as you search for small signs of a new life.
Try to follow your father's unseen course,
feeling with your gaze along the picture
rails and skirting boards where he may have paused
to leave a sweet bead of resurrection.

David Hale

Memory

The train from Schipol is a seam of light
travelling through the dusk
between snow-edged field, embankment.

Father is drinking coffee, mother holding my hand
when a man appears, dark-bearded, smiling.
He holds out a gold coin and says, *Take it, it's for you.*

I look up at father, at mother's pale face,
down at the coin—how light it is! this flat gold moon—
barely notice as the man disappears.

The train crosses into Germany
and father peels away the gold. Beneath is
chocolate, which I bite into, wondering at such alchemy.

So where there is gold, there's chocolate—
something learned on this bright holiday train.
From now on, no coin is safe from my jaws:

base metal is scraped, bitten, causing pain
and confusion. All coins are kept from my reach
till the penny drops, so to speak.

You could say I remember this. But I don't.
I am painting from memory, and someone else
is moving my hand.

C J Driver

Inside

When I was locked inside a cell
In 'Ninety Days' of solitary,
A friend would send me chocolate,
The kind that's filled with alcohol—
'Liqueurs', to be polite.

The cop who came to question me
Would check the package held no secret notes
But let the chocolates through—

And when I offered him a choice
He looked to where the secret mike was placed.
Hell, no, he winked

Then picked the 'Dark Delight'.

'Chocolate has it'

Rose Cook

It

Chocolate has it.
No-one knows why
but chocolate has it.

Like a blazing fire in winter
after building a snowman
and coming home with wet gloves,
chocolate has it.

Carob doesn't really have it.
Celery definitely doesn't have it
but chocolate, oh, chocolate has it.

Long kissing has it, babies have it,
a vase full of tulips has it.

A cup of Earl Grey tea has it (for me).
Apple pie and cream, walking out at night,
hugging a tree, all have it

though chocolate has it most.
Chocolate is queen.

Vivien Jones

Valentine's Recipe on Woman's Hour

I saw that look in your eyes,
mirrored in mine, I'm sure.
That *why shouldn't we* moment.

Two suggestions:

1. Go for a walk, hold hands,
    don't argue, eat chocolate.

2. Warm chocolate between your breasts,
    dip it in brandy and feed your lover.

The first was easy,
and so was the second.

Oliver Comins

Your Fingerprints on my Cellophane

The next time they try to write
a history of chocolate
there will be no clear and explicit reference
to this moment of fulfilment:

two creams (of mountain rose
and gorgeous violet) which teased,
then smothered, our taste buds
before they were mugged by a surge of cocoa.

Dorothy Baird

Music of the Squares

In the drawer in the hall
hiding
are three bars.

They sing
as I go past.
Such mellow voices.

I shouldn't have
had my ears dewaxed.

Pauline Prior-Pitt

70%

I like how you break up
into thirty squares

your slow melt
on my tongue

your rich glow
coating my inside cheeks

how the swallowing
the letting you go   is fine

because I know there are another
twenty nine   all mine

JoAnne McKay

Temptation

What is it makes you want me?
Stop. Think of what you could be
without your sweet smooth mouth-whore.
Want me more? Unwrap and see.

Gill Learner

Advice to a Gentleman Caller

Don't waste your cash on flowers.
Just bring me bars
of rich and dark *criollo* conched for hours.

Taste with me: let a nibble linger on your tongue,
savour fruit, spice, acidity for long
delicious moments of nuances, no single one too strong.

Sweet-talk to me of caramel, honey, pistachio, praline,
of raspberry parfait, butter-cream,
each one enrobed in 70% Single Origin.

Tell me about chemistry. How polyphenols help
prevent disease, flavenoids may stop
arteries from clogging, that my stress-levels will drop.

Teach me geography. Open up the atlas, say
the two of us will fly one day
to Ghana, Madagascar, Sâo Tomé.

Valrhona, Bonnat, Venchi are the words to murmur
to make my pulses hammer.
And if you find my tastes bizarre, blame Montezuma.

Tony Cloke

Loss

Surrounded by toffees
and bitter-sweet marzipan
I miss your soft centre.

Janet Loverseed

The Ladies from the Slimming Club Wear Black

The ladies from the slimming club wear black.
Their chocolate eyes are sad. On a day
of white meringue-froth clouds in sunny skies
they're trying to love raw veg and low-fat cheese
to enter ballrooms, thin, by Christmas Eve.

And so they do. Those lived-through, choc-free months
have done the trick. They can be golden girls,
sequinned and pink-clad. But look! They've found
such wild, wild parties, they're Dionysiac,
they're dancing in a frenzy! And in black.

Edith Ryan

Perfect Picture

auburn curls
big brown eyes

bright blue dress
angelic size

perfectly sweet
just like a doll

one chocolate bar
spoils it all

*'Irrefutable proof
that contraries co-exist'*

Marcia Menter

Salt-Caramel Logic

Irrefutable proof
that contraries coexist:

the first bite's always the best
and one bite's never enough.

Alison Brackenbury

Bournville Babies

When you start in a chocolate factory,
the teacher said (why did she glance at me?)
they say, 'Eat all you want'. After a week
they know the slightest taste will make you sick.
This may have been a story adults tell,
all confidence, no proof. Like laws. Like Hell.

For Hell, I knew then, could be chocolate.
Nougat could rot your fillings to the root.
The lemon creams (which never saw a tree)
would leave you longing for unsugared tea.
Sweet hazelnuts cracked sourly. In time
Turkish Delight would coat your tongue with slime.

I hope a quiet man, who dreams his life
through cocoa fumes, each day, at five to five,
with delicate fingers, from the whizzing line
prises his choice, then savours it like wine,
spurns toffee, nougat, rum; scoops for his treat
the Coffee Creme, which no-one else will eat.

Jim C Wilson

Dark Choku

Inside the lid
outlined in gold—
ghosts of chocolates.

Joanna Grigg

Evidence of Kindness

From the drawer: dark chocolate orange with geranium,
milk chocolate butterscotch, *tablette noir* 66%. Unwrapping
and keeping paper whole, I unstitch seams of foil, lay each
on the keyboard, watch as I would a beach of bodies naked
in the sun. Continental delicacy scored by few bare lines,
brash earthy chunks, toffee's creamy skin.

Breaking a piece, the inside's dark, the bloom of age
only surface-deep. I lick it. A memory is there, far back.
A man, caught in his imaginings, wanders past. I watch him
as he busies round, hair greying, lying in the pattern
of our recent lives, strands far apart. His face
is open like the bodies on the beach. As flavour
floods my mouth I push it round, locate tongue-side for salt,
rear for sour, the tip for sweet. He remembers too, I see.

Hilary Menos

Wakusei Shokora

I gave my sweetheart something out of this world
to show her my love transcends the earthly realm.
A box of Wakusei Shokora—chocolate planets—
from the shop in Osaka's Righa Royal Hotel.

There's a hand-made, hand-painted truffle for each planet.
I bought the whole solar system, including the sun
which is made from pineapple and Criollo cacao,
a snip on Valentine's Day at four thousand yen

(and the chance to make Uranus jokes is priceless).
More than roses, or a bottle of French perfume,
I thought her unyielding heart would be wooed by the promise
of swallowing speckled Venus or praline Neptune.

But there are only eight chocolate planets. Where is Pluto?
Surely fun-size planets are planets too?
It's been relegated to 'trans-Neptunian object'
by the International Astronomical Union (IAU).

And Saturn's rings are just lines drawn on the box.
I'd rather a retro blue-wrapped Milky Way
(my dad's yardstick of value through decimalization).
And, for that price, these things should be to scale

or at least bigger. Which is what my sweetheart said,
sucking ganache from Saturn's cappuccino eyeball.
Is this how Armstrong felt, knee deep in moon dust,
gazing up at a cloud-laced blue-green marble?

Mike Munro

Good for Something

It can't weight paper, hold the reckoning down
from the snatch of a thieving breeze.

You can't smash windows with it,
hurl it as you might,
or stop the lightest door from
a sudden shut on you.

You're about as much use, she said,
as a chocolate ashtray.

But when she's snuffed her last fag somewhere else,
I'll see that white hand open
for what will cut the sweet smoke
with a darker, bitter hit.

David Mark Williams

Bath

This is the only way to get enough.
Always that slight resistance at first,
pushing through the clean imperative.

You're hesitant, testing with one foot,
tongues of chocolate sliding between your toes.
But there you are a moment later,
standing in the sweet silt,
wary of feet slipping from under you.

Grip the sides and lower yourself in.
See how it dresses you in dark silk,
your skin gleaming with one sheen!
Sluice it over your arms.
Stroke a scarf around your neck.

Always the last to be anointed, your face
grows featureless, your hair slicked of its curls.

Jo Field

I'll say I don't like chocolate

No no, I haven't got an allergy, don't care about
my weight my teeth my skin, don't need
a substitute for sex, I'll say.

So chocolate rolls into the mouth, as smooth
and comforting as tears,

the inside of my bath is slickly smooth
but not since childhood have I felt
the urge to lick it.

I don't appreciate that fleece-clad camouflage
about the tongue, can do without those softly well
aimed punches to the tastebuds.

I'm fond of mauve, loathe the smell
of grass (these are other things I'll say).

I don't drink wine. Have never had a parking ticket
or a speeding fine. I didn't love him anyway.

Sue Butler

Hunger

When you call round, demanding
the last of your things, I make tea,
tip chocolates from a bag
into your cupped hand. They spill
until you hold just one—
a heart. We stare at
the awful power of chance. And I know
I'll never smell chocolate again
without thinking of this. Us. Bravely,
I pick it up, careful
not to touch your palm. I let it melt
on my tongue. Eat another,
another—even the spilled ones.

Outside in sleet your dark hair
is plastered to your head
as you load your car—books, socks, ties.
Two shirts escape, ghosts
in a fight. One flies down the lane.
One waves.

Jennifer Copley

Their Angel

She's sitting between Tessa and the wall.
Next to Tess, their angel's eating chocolates.
He's picked out all the milk ones, offers up the dark.
They like his furry wings, soft as teddy bears.

The sisters wonder how he gets undressed.
Perhaps he wears the same clothes all the time or has a magic zip.
Teatime comes but they're all too full of chocolate.
Their angel flies off lumpily, dropping paper shells across the floor.

They leave the front door open just in case.
Born in a field? says their mother, whose life is full
of women's meetings, coffee mornings, Sales.
She despairs of daughters, their heads always in the clouds.

'Crudbury's, Milk Decay,
Quality Shite'

Mary Wight

Rest

If a postcard had been sent
it might have read: *Wish
you were here—West Bay, Dorset.
The cliffs not so golden—
in fact wet, miserable today.*

The black wrapper had been torn,
it seemed with care, midway
between the *a* and *r*. Teeth
marks scored the chocolate, caramel
oozing across a stone now,
separated
by a few yards, glistening
rain-washed rock and for ever
pieces of a story. The man
nameless, recumbent, broken,
all his work and playing done.

Rob A Mackenzie

Chocolate Dream from Sheol

Although there is no day, no night, no rock
to climb or rumours of a distant splash,
I dream—a plutonic hub—of bitter slabs
of plain *Bone Vile* evolving from oil slick

and, badly lit within my candlebulb brain:
a shadowy rush defining borders,
a mazy hall of chocolate mirrors
reflecting Sheol's haze in solid form.

I plod as if concrete, but insubstantial
shades of passion flyby like crowmelt:
Crudbury's, Milk Decay, Quality Shite,
LOVE and HATE's hypersubtle knuckles.

Each mushrooming desire downspirals
in loops of dark, imploding squares.

Donald Mackay

Terry's

he'd thought he knew how dark can be
blacker than a blackout blind
than the land
on the shore of that dark sea

as black as black can be
until she takes his hand
and out they step into a darker land
where nothing can be told by

staring-at and yet he's happy
for she has his hand
they walk a little then they stand

a snap
of chocolate and
he can taste how sweet the dark can be

Helen Evans

Chocoholic

I've given up booze for Lent. It's my choice:
alcohol or chocolate. I can't face

losing that sugar-fuelled rush. The childhood
crème eggs licked to hollow shells and crushed

between my tongue and teeth. The adult
darkness swallowed with a glass of malt.

Then I find a woman on the ground,
half-eaten oblongs scattered by her hand—

a heart attack . . . I help with mouth-to-mouth
until the paramedic calls a halt

and I stand up, the odour on my breath,
the taste in my saliva, sickly sweet.

Martin Zarrop

Trade

Cote d'Ivoire, 2012

All day the child lifts cocoa bags
higher than a grown man.
He staggers and feels the bike chain cut
into his aching flesh.

In Mali, they promised him a bicycle.
Here, he eats corn paste, burnt bananas,
sleeps on a plank, pisses in a can
like the other eighteen.

At night, locked in this tiny room,
only his breath can escape.
Through one small hole, life enters,
more precious than chocolate.

Helena Nelson

'Dip me in chocolate and throw me to the lesbians'

The bold imperative
leaves much unanswered. For instance—
what kind of chocolate?
I think it would be couverture,
almost certainly *Lindt*.
Dark, not milk; bitter, not sweet. Still
some ambiguity—
who's the dippee? Garment? Wearer?
Wearer, I'd say, because
I am so utterly in love
with the mental picture
of smeary footprints, innocent
record of forced landing;
the victim excited but thrown,
scared of those slick quick tongues,
the brief invitation of jaws.

Helen Addy

Rita Black

Pale survivor of scarlet fever and diphtheria,
her shoulders arched against the Glasgow sky,
dark chocolate sweetening her tongue.
Black Magic was her playground name.

Sixty years later, she gave her daughter a box.
Blind to its history, the girl left it untouched.
Under the cellophane, the red ribbon tightened,
soft centres hardened into bone.

Tom Duddy

Trove

When he was a child she began to hide from him
anything sweet that had class—a rich cake,
dark chocolates, Belgian biscuits—keeping them
not selfishly, not for herself, but for the sake

of uninvited guests. He's nearly forty now,
and the pattern has not changed, except that
she forgets her hiding places. Sometimes, flecked
and blanched, chocolates are found at the back

of a cupboard, or in a bed where no one sleeps.
She, when she finds them, laughs, as if to say
I'm a terrible woman! and throws them out.
He, when he finds them, will eat them grimly.

'It used to be cocoa'

Clare Best

Hot Chocolate at Baratti's

Dark as blood, smooth as melted *fontina*,
slick on the tongue, exquisite velvet
sliding too soon, sweet-heavy,
down to the heart. Only three sips each
and already my mother is back from the dead
in her best wool coat. How we laugh,
not having seen her in years. *Ancor una*
cioccolata con panna, e un piatto
di marrons glacés, per favore. The talk
is all chocolate pudding with clotted cream,
Belgian truffles, roses and violets.

She kisses us, slips away. We wrap up
for starry streets, the pavement tilting
at such an odd angle this late afternoon
that we run through Turin
in a sugary haze (trams clanking,
bicycles skimming, aroma of chestnuts)
towards a gold sun sinking in cocoa clouds,
as if to suggest we turn and return,
spend the rest of our lives at Café Baratti
in leather chairs under brass chandeliers,
forever euphoric on chocolate and love.

John Purser

Bedtime

It used to be cocoa.

You mixed the powder with warm milk—a little
stirred and stirred to make a paste
stirred and stirred to make a mug

of cocoa. Not chocolate.

Then you—not anyone else but you—
added the sugar. You still can.
Just buy the right stuff.

OK? Now you sit down and become the ad.

You should be on an old wooden chair
at any kind of table. No, no, no—
get off the couch, this is not about sex.
This is about communion between you
and the mug and the cocoa—
no distractions, please.

All done?—but you forgot the spoon!
Look in! See there—that dark circle round the base?
That's the last mystery. You may stir to eternity,
it will always be there, that sweet and bitter taste.
It would be a shame to miss it, just before night.

Enid Lee

The Word

'But as to words; they seem to me to affect us in a manner very different from that in which we are affected by natural objects, or by painting or architecture; yet words have as considerable a share in exciting ideas of beauty and of the sublime as many of those. . . .'
  ~ Edmund Burke, in 'On the Sublime and Beautiful'

The tide's right in. You wonder
whether to take a risk.
Your feet crunch on pebbles.

Your eyes glance down,
then return to the horizon.

Your head is full—no room
for other stuff, no room for anything
but the word and this.
'Sublime.' *Sublime.*

Hot chocolate in a glass,
a long silver spoon and
I've something for you to sign.
You wonder why it hurts.

Back at the sea it's cold
but you're warmed as he holds
out his hand and you smile—
it's just like Lapis Lazuli—
a perfect blue: the very
colour of heaven.

Clifford Forde

Ode

As *Cocoa* I knew you first, my evening comforter, pressed
smooth from the bean and spun in silk webs round the rim
of cup or glass, caressing mouth and tongue. But somewhat later
came my choice of smoother fancy, winking at me from the brim
and, truly, up above the brim at bedtime's drowsy rest.

O naughty, sensuous enchantress! No, not all the famed
beans of Arabica would tempt me then, or make me wish
to wipe the dusky stain clean from these lips—that fervent kiss,
which I hold dear and sweet. Your name? O *Chocolate!* Meet
for all occasions celebratory, consolatory—amatory, in fact—
(or so they say). A treat.

Anita John

After Sledging

You come in glad from the blue light,
pull off salopettes, gloves, coat, woollen hat,
stand before me, pink-cheeked, thermal-clad,
asking for hot chocolate, marshmallows
and can you watch a video?

Milk in the pan on the stove roils
and steams. It swirls to muscovado brown,
the dragon's warming breath of cocoa.
Outside, shadows and snow.

Inside you're burrowed beneath duvets,
your laughter escaping as spindrift and flurry.
Your eyes are two circles of light,
bright as the moon in the dark of the night.

Ross Kightly

Being grown-up is

having hot chocolate and brandy
for brunch
because the breeze outside
is 'a bit nippy'.

Matthew Stewart

Chocolate con Churros

The vat of oil must haze the air,
batter must be sticky but slick.
He pipes it gently through the nozzle.
Spatulas dance as it ripples
in ring after fizzing gold ring.

Just after dawn his café steams
with hunters, half-cut teenagers
and widows, all hunched over cups
in the hubbub of the *churros*
being dunked in *chocolate*.

Robert Nye

Drinking Hot Chocolate in the Rain

Drinking some hot dark chocolate through a hole
In a cardboard cup as the bright rain came down
I saw the market and the people in it
Glorified and transfigured utterly
As if they were the very dream of God.

The chocolate in my cup held some vanilla,
A little stick, a pod I licked just once
As I stood staring at that shining scene,
Knowing that I was in it but not of it.
My tongue went out to taste the raindrops then.

There in the market by that coffee-stall
I saw the world turned inside-out. The rain
Flew upwards like so many crystal sparks
Returning to the glory of the sun
As I drank my dark chocolate to the dregs.

This, this is ecstasy, to stand and drink
Hot chocolate in the rain, lost in a crowd
Of strangers, and to feel for them such love
As Dante felt for Beatrice when he saw
Her passing by and his own heart bowed down.